# Animals of the Night

# OPOSSUMS
## AFTER DARK

### Heather M. Moore Niver

**Enslow Publishing**
101 W. 23rd Street
Suite 240
New York, NY 10011
USA
enslow.com

# Words to Know

**carnivore**—An animal that eats meat.

**iris**—The flat, colored part of the eye around the pupil.

**litter**—A group of baby animals born to an animal all at once.

**mammals**—Animals that have a backbone and hair, usually give birth to live babies, and produce milk to feed their young.

**marsupial**—A mammal that is carried and fed in a pouch in the mother's belly after birth.

**nocturnal**—Mostly active at night.

**omnivore**—An animal that eats both plants and animals.

**opposable**—Able to move and bend to touch other fingers or toes on the same hand or foot.

**prehensile**—A tail or limb that can grip or grab.

**prey**—An animal hunted by another animal for food.

**pupil**—The dark center of the eye that controls light.

# Contents

# The Joke's on Who?

In the dark forest, the leaves rustle. Following her pink nose, an opossum shuffles through the shadows. She's looking for food, but another **nocturnal** beast lurks nearby. A hungry coyote prepares to pounce. But without warning, the opossum seems to die! She is still and her body is stiff. The puzzled coyote waits. It circles the body. The opossum doesn't move. Instead, a stinking, green fluid begins to ooze from its bottom. Finally, the coyote wanders off. It will find something fresher. When the coast is clear, the opossum springs back to life. The joke's on you, coyote. This opossum was just playing dead!

## FUN FACT!

An opossum's eyes look entirely black. All we see is the black **pupil**. They do have a white **iris**, but it is very thin. Scientists think a wide pupil helps them see better at night.

The opossum's dark eyes are perfect for searching for food in the night.

# Marvelous Marsupials

Opossums are mighty interesting animals. Sometimes they are called possums. There are sixty different species, or kinds, of opossums. The most famous kind is the Virginia, or common, opossum. They are also the largest opossum.

Opossums are **mammals**. They are a special kind of mammal called a **marsupial**. Marsupials have a pouch on their belly in which to carry their young.

Baby opossums aren't fully developed when they're born, so they stay in the pouch to grow for another seven or eight weeks.

There are more than one hundred types of marsupials. Marsupials also include animals like kangaroos, koalas, and wombats. Most marsupials are found in Australia and New Guinea. The majority of opossums live in Central and South America. Virginia opossums are the only marsupials found in North America.

Opossums usually live in forests. They like areas where there are plenty of trees and water. Most opossums make their homes in dens. They might live in a hollow tree or under its roots. Some live under tree stumps. Opossums collect materials like grass to make their dens comfortable.

Opossums like living in
the forest the best.

# Look at Me!

Opossums are about the same size as an average house cat. From snout to tail they are about 2 ½ feet (76 centimeters) long. They weigh between about 9 and 13 pounds (4 and 6 kilograms).

Opossums that live in the north are usually a light gray color. In the southern areas, they might be almost black. Their noses are long and narrow. They have small black eyes and round black ears.

An opossum has rough fur covering its body.

An opossum's tail is about half the length of its body. The tail doesn't have much hair and it has scales. Opossums use their **prehensile** tails to grip branches. They can hang from their tails in the trees. But they can't sleep upside down. Opossums can use their tails to carry things, too.

Five toes and sharp claws on their front feet help them climb. On their back feet, the toes on the insides do not have claws. They are **opposable** toes that can grab branches. These toes work a lot like our thumbs.

## FUN FACT!

A group of many opossums are called a passel. Male opossums are known as jacks and females are called jills. When they are young they are called joeys, just like their kangaroo cousins.

The opossum is designed for climbing trees!

# Time to Dine

Opossums are not picky eaters. They will eat just about anything! Opossums are **omnivores**, which means they eat both plants and animals. Their diet includes insects, small mammals, eggs, fruit, and more. Opossums sometimes check out garbage cans and pick at dead animals.

Virginia opossums are on the menu for many animals. That is, they are **prey** for foxes, coyotes, snakes, and large birds. In some parts of the world, humans hunt opossums, too. In the southern United States, they are sometimes hunted for food.

This opossum has found a rat for dinner.

# Playing Possum and Other Defenses

Plenty of predators are more than happy to eat opossums. But opossums have some clever ways to defend themselves.

Sometimes they are surprised and cannot run away. So they pretend they are dead. This is sometimes called "playing possum." Opossums can act dead even if the predator bites them. They can stay like this for a minute or up to six hours! Most animals like to eat fresher meat. The predator usually decides to look for something else that is not already "dead."

## FUN FACT!

Opossums can make themselves seem sick, too. They drool and blow bubbles out of their noses. They also yell. Who wants to eat that?!

Opossums can play dead until the danger passes.

Sometimes playing dead doesn't keep the predator from attacking. If it has the chance, an opossum will run away if there is danger. When an opossum is threatened, it might show its sharp teeth. She has to stand her ground. So she flashes her fifty sharp teeth. She hisses to warn away danger.

Opossums do have a secret weapon. It's a special ingredient in their blood. It keeps them safe from the poison of animals like snakes and scorpions.

An angry or threatened opossum will hiss and show its many teeth.

Opossums are also safe from poisonous snakes like rattlesnakes and cottonmouths. In fact, opossums can eat these snakes! Scientists are studying opossum blood. They hope they can find a medicine to cure humans when they are bitten.

Opossums also have another pretty amazing defense. They rarely get a disease called rabies. Rabies can kill humans and other animals. They need to be treated right away after being bitten by an infected animal.

Opossums don't have to run from even the most poisonous rattlesnakes!

# Opossum Moms

Some old stories say that the mother opossum gives birth through her nose! But right before birth, the mother sticks her nose into her pouch. She is making sure it is clean for her new babies.

Opossums have a unique way of raising their young. When opossum babies are born, they are the size of tiny honeybees. They are blind and do not have any fur. A mother might have up to twenty-five babies. Usually only seven or eight of them survive. They crawl into the mother's pouch to continue developing.

## FUN FACT!

Opossums that live in colder areas usually give birth once a year. In warmer areas, opossum moms might have two litters a year.

Newborn opossums live and eat in the mother's pouch. This baby is
drinking milk from one of its mother's nipples.

The pouch is warm and lined with fur. The babies can drink milk from the mother's nipples. There are usually about thirteen nipples. In most opossum species, the babies stay attached for almost two months.

After the babies let go of the nipples, they are carried in the pouch. When they are too big to stay in the pouch, they climb out and ride on the mother. They hold on to her fur. At this stage, the mother can leave her babies in the den when she goes hunting. Virginia opossums can usually live on their own after one hundred days.

When they have grown too big for the pouch, young opossums hang on to their mother's fur.

# Awesome Water Opossums

One example of the many interesting kinds of opossums roaming around is the water opossum. It is known as a yapok or yapock. The water opossum is a **carnivore**, so it only eats meat. It has webs of skin between its toes that help with swimming. Oily fur helps it slip through the water, too. Its pouch tightens up to keep its babies dry. Water opossums live in South America.

## FUN FACT!

One of the smallest opossums is the short-tailed opossum. Most are only about 4 inches (11 cm) long, including the tail. They are also known for having small eyes.

Water opossums are the only marsupials that spend part of their lives in the water!

# Thank You, Opossum!

Opossums are good to have around. They eat snails, slugs, and beetles, which are not good for humans' gardens. Opossums can also keep rats and cockroaches away. They hunt for the same foods, so the pests move somewhere else. Opossums have a great memory. They can always remember where they found a good place to eat!

Opossums also kill ticks. Ticks are insects that can pass nasty diseases on to humans. They bite, lick, and scratch the ticks off their fur. They might kill four thousand ticks in one week!

This young opossum will soon grow up and help humans by eating pests that would destroy gardens or pass on disease.

# Stay Safe Around Opossums

Opossums usually are relaxed and don't want to be near humans. But sometimes they wander too near where we live and play. Follow these tips to stay safe around these wild animals:

- Keep tight lids on garbage cans. Opossums don't usually bother garbage, but if another animal makes a mess, opossums might come by to see what is left.

- Never keep an opossum as a pet. They are wild animals.

- Don't leave pet food outside. Opossums can sniff that out and may eat it. If you have fruit trees, pick up fallen fruit.

- If you think an opossum is living in a hole under your deck, fill it with loose material, like crumpled paper or straw. The opossum will push it out of the way. If nothing happens, it is safe to fill in the hole.

- If you realize you have an opossum living in a hole, wait a couple hours after dark. By then the opossum should be out. Then you can fill the hole with dirt or other loose material.

# Learn More

## Books

Green, Emily K. *Opossums*. Minneapolis: Bellwether Media, 2011.

Hicks, Kelli L. *Nocturnal Animals*. North Mankato, MN: Capstone Press, 2012.

McGill, Jordan. *Opossums*. New York: Weigl Publishers, 2012.

Tatlock, Ann. *Opossums*. Kennett Square, PA: Purple Toad Publishing, 2015.

Webster, Christine. *Opossums*. New York: Weigl Publishers, 2013.

## Websites

**National Wildlife Federation: Ranger Rick**
**nwf.org/Kids/Ranger-Rick/Animals/Mammals/Opossums.**
**aspx**
> Get to know how an opossum lives, as told through the words of "Perry Opossum."

**Opossum Society of the United States**
**opossumsocietyus.org**
> Learn all about opossums with facts and photos.

**San Diego Zoo Kids**
**kids.sandiegozoo.org/animals/mammals/opossum**
> Photos and facts help tell the story of the awesome opossum.

# Index

Published in 2016 by Enslow Publishing, LLC.
101 W. 23rd Street, Suite 240, New York, NY 10011

Copyright © 2016 by Enslow Publishing, LLC.

**Library of Congress Cataloging-in-Publication Data**

Niver, Heather M. Moore.
Opossums after dark / by Heather M. Moore Niver.
  p. cm. — (Animals of the night)
Includes bibliographical references and index.
ISBN 978-0-7660-7304-3 (library binding)
ISBN 978-0-7660-7302-9 (pbk.)
ISBN 978-0-7660-7303-6 (6-pack)
1. Opossums — Juvenile literature. 2. Nocturnal animals — Juvenile literature. I. Niver, Heather Moore. II. Title.
QL737.M34N58 2015
599.2'76—d23

Printed in the United States of America

**To Our Readers:** We have done our best to make sure all website addresses in this book were active and appropriate when we went to press. However, the author and the publisher have no control over and assume no liability for the material available on those websites or on any websites they may link to. Any comments or suggestions can be sent by e-mail to customerservice@enslow.com.

**Photos Credits:** Throughout book, narvikk/E+/Getty Images (starry background), kimberrywood/Digital Vision Vectors/Getty Images (green moon dingbat); cover, p. 1 Becky Sheridan/Shutterstock.com (opossum), samxmed/E+/Getty Images (moon); p. 3 Brian Lasenby/Shutterstock.com; p. 5 David Courtenay/Oxford Scientific/Getty Images; p. 7 S.J. Krasemann/Photo Library/Getty Images; p. 9 Rex Lisman/iStock/Thinkstock; p. 11 Purestock/Thinkstock; p. 13 Steve Maslowski/Science Source/Getty Images; p. 15 vkuzmin/iStock/Thinkstock; p. 17 Stacy Barnett/Shutterstock.com; p. 19 Rex Lisman/iStock/Thinkstock; p. 21 Karine Aigner/National Geographic/Getty Images; p. 23 John Cancalosi/Photolibrary/Getty Images; p. 25 Frank Lukasseck/Photographer's Choice/Getty Images; p. 27 Jon Hall www.mammalwatching.com; p. 29 Tim Harman/Shutterstock.com.